The Journey to the Cross and Beyond

Stations around Lindisfarne

by Mary Fleeson

The Stations of the Cross are a series of images that tell the story of the events leading up to, and sometimes including, the resurrection. The images are often presented alongside prayers and meditations and are intended to provide a preparation for Easter Day.

Entering the Season of Lent can be an amazing journey of discovery, an opportunity to journey to the foot of the cross, to be challenged by the sacrifice and reassured by the resurrection. The Stations in this book will, I hope, guide and help you in that journey, they follow the 'Scriptural Way of the Cross' developed by Pope John Paul ll, with the addition of the resurrection (He is Risen) and are set around the village of Lindisfarne, Northumbria, UK. I have chosen to place this ancient and terrible journey around my home village but the meditations and prayers included could be used anywhere (you could find places around your own house or town or garden) and the book can also be used whilst sitting quietly.

With every blessing,
Mary Fleeson

About this book

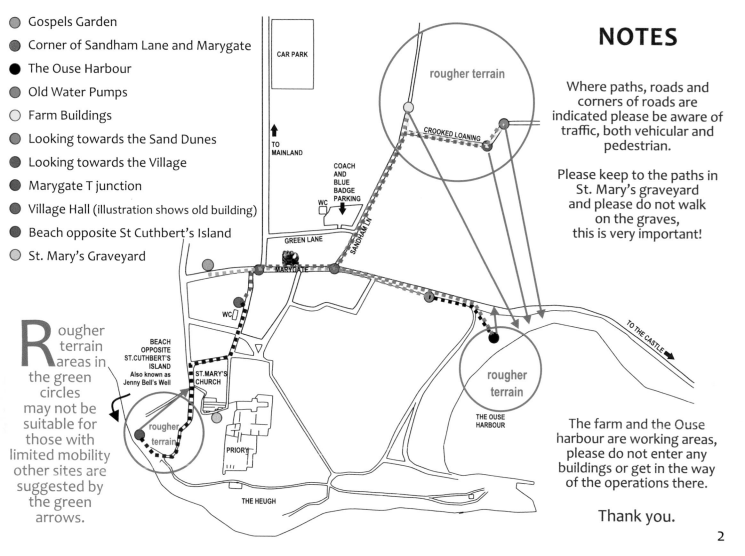

- Gospels Garden
- Corner of Sandham Lane and Marygate
- The Ouse Harbour
- Old Water Pumps
- Farm Buildings
- Looking towards the Sand Dunes
- Looking towards the Village
- Marygate T junction
- Village Hall (illustration shows old building)
- Beach opposite St Cuthbert's Island
- St. Mary's Graveyard

NOTES

Where paths, roads and corners of roads are indicated please be aware of traffic, both vehicular and pedestrian.

Please keep to the paths in St. Mary's graveyard and please do not walk on the graves, this is very important!

Rougher terrain areas in the green circles may not be suitable for those with limited mobility other sites are suggested by the green arrows.

The farm and the Ouse harbour are working areas, please do not enter any buildings or get in the way of the operations there.

Thank you.

CAR PARK

TO MAINLAND

COACH AND BLUE BADGE PARKING

rougher terrain

CROOKED LOANING

SANDHAM LN

GREEN LANE

MARYGATE

WC

WC

BEACH OPPOSITE ST.CUTHBERT'S ISLAND Also known as Jenny Bell's Well

ST.MARY'S CHURCH

rougher terrain

PRIORY

THE HEUGH

rougher terrain

THE OUSE HARBOUR

TO THE CASTLE

2

At the start of each Station say:

Creator of all things
immense and invisible
and everything in-between,
Creator of me,
Hear my call.

Send Your Spirit into my heart,
I bind it there
to teach me how to love,

Send Your Spirit into my
mind, I bind it there
to guide me,

Send Your Spirit into my
body, I bind it there
to sustain me.

Creator God, Hear my call.

Prayers to use at each Station

At the end of each Station:

Thank You
Awesome God,
For loving me.

Thank You
Eternal God,
For teaching me.

Thank You
Merciful God,
For saving me.

Contents

Gethsemane

Then Jesus went with his disciples to a place called Gethsemane, and he said to them, 'Sit here while I go over there and pray.' He took Peter and the two sons of Zebedee along with him, and he began to be sorrowful and troubled. Then he said to them, 'My soul is overwhelmed with sorrow to the point of death. Stay here and keep watch with me.'

Going a little farther, he fell with his face to the ground and prayed, 'My Father, if it is possible, may this cup be taken from me. Yet not as I will, but as you will.'

Then he returned to his disciples and found them sleeping. 'Couldn't you men keep watch with me for one hour?' he asked Peter. 'Watch and pray so that you will not fall into temptation. The spirit is willing, but the flesh is weak.'

He went away a second time and prayed, 'My Father, if it is not possible for this cup to be taken away unless I drink it, may your will be done.'

When he came back, he again found them sleeping, because their eyes were heavy. So he left them and went away once more and prayed the third time, saying the same thing.

Then he returned to the disciples and said to them, 'Are you still sleeping and resting? Look, the hour has come, and the Son of Man is delivered into the hands of sinners. Rise! Let us go! Here comes my betrayer!'

Matthew 26:36-46

meditate

And when I'm weary You are there,
Lifting my burdens.

Would I have slept while you prayed
in the garden that night?

And when I'm scared You hold my hand,
Reassuring my thoughts.

Would I have prayed while you cried
in the garden that night?

And when I'm overwhelmed You give me light,
Illuminating my days.

Would I have cried when You left
the garden that night?

pray

Loving God,

Sometimes I only want
to hide myself
in the dreamless sleep
of avoidance,
sometimes the reality
of life seems too much
to bear...

Show me, creator God,
the wonders
of this world,
the life and love and hope
that thrives in Your light.
And when I cry out,
at the times I cannot see,
Hear me and hold me,

Loving God.

● Gospels Garden

Tread gently
amidst
the twittering
birds, listen
closely
to their songs,
touch a petal
or a leaf,
let its softness
soothe you,
sniff the Island
air, tinged with
salt,

sit a while
and breathe.

The Kiss

While he was still speaking, Judas, one of the Twelve, arrived. With him was a large crowd armed with swords and clubs, sent from the chief priests and the elders of the people. Now the betrayer had arranged a signal with them:

'The one I kiss is the man; arrest him.'

Going at once to Jesus, Judas said, 'Greetings, Rabbi!' and kissed him.

Jesus replied, 'Do what you came for, friend.'

Matthew 26:47-49

meditate

*He called him friend,
Confidant, companion, ally, chum.*

*He called him friend.
Despite the kiss, despite the sting.*

*Despite the betrayal that must have hurt,
Even through the knowledge
Of prophecy fulfilled,
In that kiss,
In that respectful greeting.*

Teacher.

Friend.

pray

My Teacher, my Friend,
May Your mission
and words of life
inspire me today,
May I learn how to live
in Your presence.

My Teacher, my Friend,
May Your pain
and sacrifice
challenge me today,
May I love unconditionally
with Your help.

Corner of Sandham Lane and Marygate

At this corner remember
other corners,
times when good things
have been there,
or unpleasant things have lurked.

Remember that
beyond each corner
lies a new perspective,
a fresh view, an unfamiliar road.

Remember the promise:
'I am with you always,
to the very end...'

The Sanhedrin

Those who had arrested Jesus took him to Caiaphas the high priest, where the teachers of the law and the elders had assembled. But Peter followed him at a distance, right up to the courtyard of the high priest. He entered and sat down with the guards to see the outcome.

The chief priests and the whole Sanhedrin were looking for false evidence against Jesus so that they could put him to death. But they did not find any, though many false witnesses came forward.

Finally two came forward and declared, 'This fellow said, "I am able to destroy the temple of God and rebuild it in three days."'

Then the high priest stood up and said to Jesus, 'Are you not going to answer? What is this testimony that these men are bringing against you?' But Jesus remained silent.

The high priest said to him, 'I charge you under oath by the living God: Tell us if you are the Messiah, the Son of God.'

'You have said so,' Jesus replied. 'But I say to all of you: from now on you will see the Son of Man sitting at the right hand of the Mighty One and coming on the clouds of heaven.'

Then the high priest tore his clothes and said, 'He has spoken blasphemy! Why do we need any more witnesses? Look, now you have heard the blasphemy. What do you think?'

'He is worthy of death,' they answered.

Then they spat in his face and struck him with their fists. Others slapped him and said, 'Prophesy to us, Messiah. Who hit you?'

Matthew 26:57-67

meditate

If I had been in that crowd,
I'd like to think
I would have defended you,
I'd like to think
that I would have spoken out,
shouted, cried, yelled, hollered
bellowed in Your defence.

If I had been in that crowd,
Would I have been willing
to admit allegiance?
Willing to be marked
as friend of a criminal?
Blasphemer! Troublemaker!
Traitor! Sorcerer! Even that!

If I had been in that crowd,
I'd like to think
that I would have defended you,
I'd like to think
that I wouldn't have run away.
If I had been in that crowd.

pray

When I see injustice,
Help me to stop it.
When the holiness of
life is defiled,
Help me to speak out.
When Your temple
is corrupted,
Help me to heal
unconditionally.

● **The Ouse**

Millions of pebbles
glistening like jewels
each one unique,
shaped by its fellows
and the tide.

Millions of people
each one precious
and unique,
shaped by their fellows
and circumstance.

Find one pebble, one that
somehow speaks to you,
hold it and remember...

...the very hairs of your head
are all numbered. Don't be
afraid; you are worth more
than many sparrows.

Pilate

Meanwhile Jesus stood before the governor, and the governor asked him, 'Are you the king of the Jews?'

'You have said so,' Jesus replied.

When he was accused by the chief priests and the elders, he gave no answer. Then Pilate asked him, 'Don't you hear the testimony they are bringing against you?' But Jesus made no reply, not even to a single charge – to the great amazement of the governor.

Now it was the governor's custom at the festival to release a prisoner chosen by the crowd. At that time they had a well-known prisoner whose name was Jesus Barabbas. So when the crowd had gathered, Pilate asked them, 'Which one do you want me to release to you: Jesus Barabbas, or Jesus who is called the Messiah?' For he knew it was out of self-interest that they had handed Jesus over to him.

While Pilate was sitting on the judge's seat, his wife sent him this message: 'Don't have anything to do with that innocent man, for I have suffered a great deal today in a dream because of him.'

But the chief priests and the elders persuaded the crowd to ask for Barabbas and to have Jesus executed.

'Which of the two do you want me to release to you?' asked the governor. 'Barabbas,' they answered.

What shall I do, then, with Jesus who is called the Messiah?' Pilate asked.

They all answered, 'Crucify him!'

'Why? What crime has he committed?' asked Pilate.

But they shouted all the louder, 'Crucify him!'

When Pilate saw that he was getting nowhere, but that instead an uproar was starting, he took water and washed his hands in front of the crowd. 'I am innocent of this man's blood,' he said. 'It is your responsibility!'

All the people answered, 'His blood is on us and on our children!'

Then he released Barabbas to them. But he had Jesus flogged, and handed him over to be crucified. **Matthew 27:11-26**

meditate

Jesus Barabbas.
Yeshua Bar Abba,
Jesus, son of the father,
Well known prisoner.
Rabble rouser.
Murderer.
Unexpected winner.
Barabbas.

Jesus, Son of God.
Yeshua Bar Abba,
Jesus, Son of the Father,
Well known teacher.
Crowd gatherer.
Healer.
Prophesied redeemer.
Jesus.

pray

May I hesitate before I condemn,
May I pause before I judge.
Let all that makes me who I am
Crave truth
and long for justice.

As I decide each moment
to choose to follow
You,

May I have the courage,
May I have the strength,
To be the person
you created me to be,
To face the crowd.

Old Water Pumps

Nowadays you won't even be able to wash your hands here but once upon a time the clanking handles would be heard from dawn to dusk, every drop of water for drinking and washing and cooking would have come from here.

Pilate literally washed his hands of responsibility for Jesus' death but Jesus used water as an analogy for the life giving Spirit of God:

...'Everyone who drinks this water will be thirsty again, but whoever drinks the water I give them will never thirst. Indeed, the water I give them will become in them a spring of water welling up to eternal life.'

Peter

Now Peter was sitting out in the courtyard, and a servant-girl came to him. 'You also were with Jesus of Galilee,' she said.

But he denied it before them all. 'I don't know what you're talking about,' he said.

Then he went out to the gateway, where another servant-girl saw him and said to the people there, 'This fellow was with Jesus of Nazareth.'

He denied it again, with an oath: 'I don't know the man!'

After a little while, those standing there went up to Peter and said, 'Surely you are one of them; your accent gives you away.'

Then he began to call down curses, and he swore to them, 'I don't know the man!'

Immediately a cock crowed. Then Peter remembered the word Jesus had spoken: 'Before the cock crows, you will disown me three times.' And he went outside and wept bitterly.

Matthew 26:69-74

meditate

What fear must have filled you to deny the friendship of your teacher companion?
What guilt-filled tears you must have shed,
when the raucous crowing announced the dawn.
What a night of sorrow.
What a night of lies.

And the fear that filled you ruins friendships today between humans.
Humans who deny the equality of humanity,
that we are all God's children, beautifully made.
What a legacy of sorrows.
What an aeon of fear.

Yet the fear that overwhelms us is truly conquered by our Saviour Friend.
The sacrifice made once was for all,
no exceptions, no discrimination, no one before another.
What a legacy of joy.
What a gift of hope.

pray

Circle me Loving God,
Keep me joyful
when sorrow surrounds me.

Circle me Creator God,
Keep me hopeful
when fear floods through me.

Circle me Merciful God,
Keep me faithful
when doubt may destroy me.

Farm Buildings

Anyone who isn't a morning person and has been woken in the early hours by the strident cacophony of cock crows will know what a piercing and jarring sound it is. Peter's nerves must have been heightened to the point where any discordant sound would be like nails on a blackboard, determinedly trying to drive him beyond the edge of sanity.
What pushes you to the edges?
Ask God to help you to cope with those things.

14

The Crown

Then the governor's soldiers took Jesus into the Praetorium and gathered the whole company of soldiers round him.

They stripped him and put a scarlet robe on him, and then twisted together a crown of thorns and set it on his head.

They put a staff in his right hand.

Then they knelt in front of him and mocked him. 'Hail, king of the Jews!' they said.

They spat on him, and took the staff and struck him on the head again and again.

Then they led him away to crucify him.

Matthew 27:27-30

Hey, soldier!
Did you volunteer to twist those thorns?
Were your fingers sore and bloodied?
Your arms scratched and torn?
Did you look at the scars later and understand?
Did you understand what you had done?

Hey, you!
Did you stand by while they spat on Him?
Did you see how they beat Him?
Or did you look the other way?
Did you think that your objections would never be heard?
Did you understand what you had done?

Hey, world!
How long can we stand by and watch?
As our Saviour in the guise of the poor,
the oppressed, the rejected, the homeless,
the lonely, the ones on the edges, continue to be ignored?
Do we understand what we are doing?

pray

Help me to understand
how I can be Your voice in the world.

Help me to know
what I should shout about in this world.

Help me to understand.

Looking Towards The Dunes

You can't get lost
in the dunes,
just go
to a high point.

But in the sandy valleys
you can feel
utterly
lost and alone.

When you are low where
are the places you go?
Who are the people that
lift you up?

Pray for them.

Carrying The Cross

Then they led him away to crucify him.

Matthew 27:31

meditate

He was strong, a carpenter would be.
Wouldn't he?
But no Superman or Hulk,
no supernatural healing
from the beating
and the whipping.
He could've done, healed that is,
and made the wooden bar as light as air.
Couldn't He?
But no,
He bore that burden of wood and souls
as a human.
No more,
no less.

pray

Thank
You
Jesus.

Looking Towards The Village

Pray for your community,
your home,
your family,
your place of work,
your places of rest.

Pray for the cities,
the hubs,
the lost,
the homeless,
the refugee.

Pray for the country,
the spaces,
the peace,
the places neglected,
the places forgotten.

Pray for the Island,
the seekers,
the pilgrims,
the working,
the living.

Pray for glimpses of heaven,
in the ordinary,
in the faces,
in the places,
in the conversations,
and the wide open skies.

18

Simon

As they were going out, they met a man from Cyrene, named Simon, and they forced him to carry the cross.

Matthew 27:32

meditate

I wonder if they had to force you Simon?
Or if you did it willingly,
somehow aware
that you were part
of a bigger picture.

I wonder if you could feel the weight
of more than just the wooden bar
on your shoulder?
Somehow aware
of the bigger picture.

I wonder if I were to take your burden,
step into your shoes for a while,
or if you wore mine,
whether we could share
a bigger picture.

Marygate
T Junction

At this point please don't block the traffic;
cars,
lorries,
people...
...parents with push-chairs,
folks with dogs,
with binoculars
and cameras,
delivery people,
builders,
locals and visitors.
Keep out of the way
but silently, subtly pray,
for them.

Then do the same
when you are home.

pray

Help me to bear the burdens of others
But not to carry them alone,
Help me to bear the burdens of others
And to lift them to You.

20

The Women

A large number of people followed him, including women who mourned and wailed for him. Jesus turned and said to them, "Daughters of Jerusalem, do not weep for me; weep for yourselves and for your children. For the time will come when you will say, 'Blessed are the childless women, the wombs that never bore and the breasts that never nursed!' Then "they will say to the mountains, 'Fall on us!' and to the hills, 'Cover us!' " For if people do these things when the tree is green, what will happen when it is dry?"

Luke 23:28-31

meditate

I was just a child, hiding behind my Mother's skirts
Watching the soldiers and the man with the cross
His eyes met mine just as he stumbled
I will never forget those eyes.

I was so scared, my Mother was weeping and wailing
Watching as the soldiers gave the cross to another
The man with the eyes paused nearby
He spoke and she listened.

I didn't catch the whole exchange with Mother
Watching, I saw her expression change, harden
The man was shoved onwards, upwards
We didn't follow the crowd.

I was about to marry when my Mother told me
Half watching the door for my Father's return
The man with the eyes, he was Jesus
Messiah, holy one.

I believed and was glad that my Mother had acted
Waiting for a match for me from far away
A man who will take me from danger
From the city that will burn.

pray

Sometimes it's hard to live in the present
when the future looms
with it's unknowable terrors
and inevitable fears.

Help me Dear Lord
to place those worries into Your hands,
to live fearlessly,
to trust that when times are difficult
You will be with me.

Village Hall
(illustration shows the old building)

As you will see, the old Village Hall has gone, to be replaced by a new, glossy, glassy, purpose built building. The old has gone, the new is here!

However the memories of happy events in the old hall still linger and the new hall is still trying to fit in and enter into the heart of the community.

The past will always inform our present and our future and sometimes it will hold us back and prevent us from embracing the new...

What memories could be holding you back today?

Place them in God's hands.

The Nails

When they came to the place called the Skull, they crucified him there, along with the criminals – one on his right, the other on his left. Jesus said, 'Father, forgive them, for they do not know what they are doing.' And they divided up his clothes by casting lots.

Luke 23:33-34

As the nails were hammered,
Echoing in the eerie stillness
of the quiet before the storm,
Sunlight may have pierced the clouds
Puncturing the gathering gloom.

As the nails were hammered,
Echoing in the eerie stillness
of the quiet before the storm,
The sky may have wept,
Tears of rain from a stormy sky.

As the nails were hammered,
Echoing in the eerie stillness
of the quiet before the storm,
The wind may have whispered
'What have they done?'

pray

May Your words be heard
and built upon,
as the love that they teach
become foundations.

May my actions and words
build Your church,
as the nails and wood
in the carpenters hands.

Beach opposite St Cuthbert's Island

The beach opposite St. Cuthbert's Island, also known as Jenny Bell's Well, is my favourite place on the Island. I have spent many peaceful hours there; watching the seals bobbing about, trying to guess where they will pop up next, listening to their songs. I have refreshed my spirit there, wept there, laughed there, played and beach-combed. To me it is a little taste of heaven.

Imagining the crucifixion is a painful and difficult thing to do, even harder perhaps in a place so distant from Golgotha, and yet even here there is a cross, erected decades ago as a memorial and a reminder of the resurrection after the terrible death of Jesus.

As you pause here be silent, contemplate the sacrifice taken and the agony suffered, this is part of our story as people who seek to be followers of Jesus.

The Thieves

One of the criminals who hung there hurled insults at him: 'Aren't you the Messiah? Save yourself and us!'

But the other criminal rebuked him. 'Don't you fear God,' he said, 'since you are under the same sentence? We are punished justly, for we are getting what our deeds deserve. But this man has done nothing wrong.'

Then he said, 'Jesus, remember me when you come into your kingdom.'

Jesus answered him, 'Truly I tell you, today you will be with me in paradise.'

Luke 23:39-43

meditate

This man has done nothing wrong!
Only spread his treasonous claims...
Nothing wrong at all!
Only spoken blasphemy out loud...
But it's not like he killed anyone,
and what is sedition anyway?
Nothing wrong!
He wasn't a thief
or a slave
or a prisoner of war
or a deserting soldier.
So why all the fuss?
Oh, I see, I get it now.
Make an example of the man who preaches love,
Love that conquers all,

Even them.

pray

Jesus remember me when you come into Your kingdom.

Beach opposite St Cuthbert's Island

Close your eyes and listen to the birds calling,
to the ancient winds
and the endless waves.

Close your eyes and listen
in your imagination,
to the laboured breathing
and the raspy conversation.

Close your eyes and listen
to the hopeful request,
to the joyful promise
that remains today.

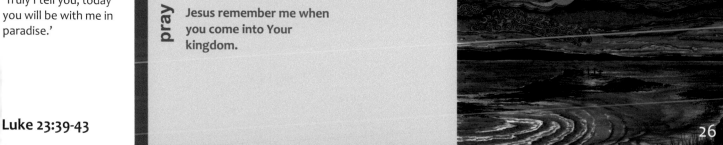

26

Mother and Son

When Jesus saw his mother there, and the disciple whom he loved standing near by, he said to her, 'Woman, here is your son,' and to the disciple, 'Here is your mother.' From that time on, this disciple took her into his home.

John 19:26-27

meditate

I nursed Him,
I fed Him and clothed Him and raised Him,
I kissed His face,
I wiped His tears and worried about Him,
I loved Him.

My precious, miraculous son,
My precocious, wise son,
My loving, amazing son.
I love Him.
I cannot look.
I cannot turn away.
I cannot see through my tears.

I followed Him,
He fed my soul and clothed me in peace,
I believed Him.
He opened my eyes to the truth,
I loved Him.

My Master, wonderful teacher,
My companion, steadfast friend,
My Lord, my Saviour,
I love him.
I cannot look.
I cannot turn away.
I cannot see through my tears.

pray

When I ponder the sacrifice You made,
Your love for us.
It is overwhelming.
Thank You.

Beach opposite St Cuthbert's Island

Two things always puzzled me about this passage, why Jesus called his Mother 'woman' as a form of address and why Jesus entrusted her care to John and not his brothers.

The first is understood to be a case of 'lost in translation', that the original meaning would have been more like Ma'am, a respectful term but not without affection.

The second is because Jesus' brothers were not present at the crucifixion and didn't become believers until after the resurrection, so John, who had been closer to Jesus during His ministry, was an obvious choice.

Consider how easy it can be to form opinions when we don't know the full story or when we have misinterpreted what we know.

My God, my God

From noon until three in the afternoon darkness came over all the land. About three in the afternoon Jesus cried out in a loud voice, 'Eli, Eli, lema sabachthani?' (which means 'My God, my God, why have you forsaken me?').

Matthew 27:45-46

Jesus called out with a loud voice, 'Father, into your hands I commit my spirit.'

Luke 23:46

Jesus said, 'It is finished.' With that, he bowed his head and gave up his spirit.

John 19:30

meditate

It is finished...
No, it's really not.
Everything has just begun.
All that You taught,
All that You gave,
Your triumph over death,
Your miraculous return.
Just the beginning...

**Beach opposite
St Cuthbert's
Island**

From Matthew's telling of the crucifixion it seems that for the time of the darkness, for those three hours Jesus wasn't able to converse with God the Father, perhaps he was in so much pain that He couldn't hear or perhaps if God had intervened in any way to offer comfort the sacrifice would have been less profound.

There are times when we feel that God is absent, too lofty to be concerned with our tiny existence but perhaps we are too much in pain to hear... the sacrifice of separation was made on our behalf by Jesus, so God is not absent to us... ever.

pray

**My God, my God,
please do not leave me.
You were at my beginning,
You breathed Your Spirit into me
And made me Your child.
Be at my ending here on earth
however it may finish
And bring me to a new beginning
with You.**

The Tomb

As evening approached, there came a rich man from Arimathea, named Joseph, who had himself become a disciple of Jesus. Going to Pilate, he asked for Jesus' body, and Pilate ordered that it be given to him. Joseph took the body, wrapped it in a clean linen cloth, and placed it in his own new tomb that he had cut out of the rock. He rolled a big stone in front of the entrance to the tomb and went away.

Matthew 27:57-60

meditate

Darkness of the tomb,
Freshness of the grave clothes,
A body battered and broken,
An ending so cruel.

Silence of the tomb,
Not a breath to be heard,
A shell of a man left behind,
An ending of purpose.

Coldness of the tomb,
Hardness of the stone ledge,
A life abused and taken,
An ending too soon.

pray

In the darkness, protect me,
In the silence, speak to me,
In the coldness, hold me.

St.Mary's Graveyard

Please don't walk on the graves, some are very old and some contain relatives of folk still living here.
There are corners around the church where you can shelter from the wind or the porch has seats if it's raining...

Remember, in this quiet place, those you loved who have left this earth-bound life.
Offer thanks for the impact they had on you.

He Is Risen

'You are looking for Jesus the Nazarene, who was crucified. He has risen! He is not here. See the place where they laid him. But go, tell his disciples and Peter, "He is going ahead of you into Galilee. There you will see him, just as he told you."'

meditate

He has risen!
Just as was prophesied,
Just as was promised.

He has risen!
The story goes on,
The story eternal.

He has risen!
Rejoice!
Rejoice!

pray

Within Your presence
Today I rejoice
In Your victory over death
Embraced by Your light
Today I live
In Your promise of life
With Your help
Today I go forward
In Your power

St.Mary's Graveyard

He is RISEN!
Smile, laugh, sing!

The empty tomb, the Son resurrected,
This is the why of why we believe.

The promise made, life beyond death,
This is the what of what we believe.

The love unconditional, no strings attached,
This is the how of how we believe.

The God in all things, Father, Son, Spirit,
This is the who of who we believe.

34

We have made all of the stations from this book available on various printed media via RedBubble.com

Visit www.lindisfarne-scriptorium.co.uk/stations for more information.

Where to get prints

Further copies of this book can be obtained through our website www.lindisfarne-scriptorium.co.uk